ADRIANA LUNA CARLOS
Editor-In-Chief, Designer
and Co-Founder

HANNA OLIVAS
Managing Editor
& Co-Founder

NICOLE CURTIS
Director of the SRS
Magazine Division

THE SCOOP

SHE RISES
STUDIOS

**ADVERTISING
OPPORTUNITIES**
Info@SheRisesStudios.com

THE SCOOP MAGAZINE
MARCH 2025

CONTACT US
SheRisesStudios@gmail.com
www.SheRisesStudios.com

www.SheRisesStudios.com

LETTER FROM THE EDITORS

Dear Readers,

March is a time of celebration, reflection, and empowerment as we honor Women's History Month—a moment to recognize the pioneers, visionaries, and changemakers who have shaped industries and redefined culture. This special edition of The Scoop Magazine is dedicated to the *Icons of Influence: Celebrating Women Who Define Beauty, Fashion, and Entertainment.* These are the women who don't just follow trends; they set them. They challenge norms, break barriers, and leave an undeniable mark on the world.

At the heart of this issue is our cover feature, Kathy Copcutt, a powerhouse in entertainment, lifestyle, and media. From publicist to nationwide TV host, lifestyle creator and travel enthusiast, Kathy embodies the essence of reinvention, resilience, and influence. Her ability to seamlessly navigate the worlds of television, luxury travel, and brand partnerships is a testament to her authenticity and passion. She's not just shaping the conversation—she's leading it.

Beyond Kathy's incredible journey, this edition is filled with stories of trailblazing women who are revolutionizing beauty, fashion, and entertainment. From the red carpets to behind-the-scenes innovation, we're spotlighting the creatives, designers, and visionaries pushing boundaries and redefining what it means to be iconic. These pages are an invitation to celebrate their artistry, courage, and unwavering determination.

As you turn the pages of this issue, we hope you feel inspired to embrace your own influence and style—because every woman has the power to make an impact. Thank you for joining us in honoring the voices and visions that continue to shape our world.

Warm regards,

Adriana Luna Carlos and Hanna Olivas
Editors of The Scoop Magazine

SHE RISES STUDIOS

FENIX TV

she wins

NICE GIRLS FINISH FIRST

SHE WINS
VIRTUAL SUMMIT 2025

When: May 14–16, 2025
Where: Exclusively on FENIX TV
Tickets: $49.97

Join us for the **She Wins Virtual Summit 2025**, a 3-day event celebrating women entrepreneurs and leaders from around the world. This year's theme, **"Nice Girls Finish First,"** showcases how kindness, empathy, and integrity drive success in business and life.

What to Expect:

- Inspiring stories from women leaders.
- Expert advice on leadership, resilience, and growth.
- Strategies for thriving in business without compromising values.

BE PART OF THIS EMPOWERING MOVEMENT AND DISCOVER HOW KINDNESS LEADS TO GREATNESS!

KATHY COPCUTT: INSPIRING AUDIENCES THROUGH TV, TRAVEL, AND AUTHENTIC LIVING

Kathy Copcutt's career is a testament to the power of adaptability, passion, and an openness to life's unexpected turns. Beginning her professional journey as an Estée Lauder Account Coordinator, she has since worn many hats, including Real Estate and Insurance Agent, Events Planner, Publicist, and, most notably, a Nationwide TV Host and Lifestyle Creator. Despite her diverse career path, one thing has remained constant: her ability to embrace change and step into new opportunities with enthusiasm.

Kathy always harbored a desire to be on television, though she never quite knew how it would come to fruition. The Yiddish saying, *"Man plans, and God laughs,"* resonates deeply with her journey. She has learned the importance of going with the flow, staying open to new possibilities, and trusting the universe. Sometimes, stepping into the unknown with faith and determination is all it takes to carve out a new path. This philosophy has been a guiding force in her life, allowing her to pivot seamlessly and embrace every challenge as an opportunity.

Pivotal Moments in Her Journey
Kathy's transition into television happened serendipitously—she filled in for someone at the last minute and found herself in front of the camera. Instantly, she fell in love with the experience. The warmth of the team, the dynamic environment, and the ability to engage with an audience all solidified her desire to be part of the industry. The connections she has built with her colleagues and viewers have made her journey even more rewarding. The TV stations she collaborates with feel like family, and every appearance is a chance to share her passions with a community that welcomes her with open arms.

Experiencing the Emmys
As both a publicist and a TV host, Kathy has had the privilege of experiencing the Emmys from multiple perspectives. The energy of Emmys week is electric, filled with awe-inspiring moments as Hollywood's finest celebrate television's best. Throughout the year, she works with studios to promote films and series that leave a lasting impact. Seeing these projects recognized on such a grand stage is incredibly fulfilling.

Beyond the awards, Kathy cherishes the camaraderie and excitement that come with the festivities. The Emmys represent not just excellence in entertainment but also a celebration of storytelling, creativity, and the collective efforts of talented individuals who bring unforgettable characters to life.

Trends in the Television Industry
While every nominee at the Emmys brings something special to the screen, Kathy has observed a growing spirit of kindness, collaboration, and support, particularly among women in the industry. It is inspiring to witness creators and actors lifting each other up, acknowledging one another's contributions, and crafting meaningful, thought-provoking content.

Rather than predicting winners, Kathy focuses on the artistry behind each performance. Whether viewers love or despise a character, the ability of an actor to evoke such strong emotions is a testament to their talent and dedication.

The Creative Process Behind Lifestyle Content

As a lifestyle creator, Kathy is highly selective about the brands and products she endorses. She believes in promoting only what she genuinely uses and trusts. Her goal is to create content that not only informs but also fosters social connections. Research shows that positive social interactions enhance both mental and physical well-being, and Kathy strives to cultivate a space where people feel connected and supported.

Her creative process is driven by authenticity, audience engagement, and a commitment to making a positive impact. By sharing her experiences and recommendations, she hopes to add value to her audience's lives while fostering a sense of community.

The Evolving Media Industry

The rise of social media has transformed the media industry in profound ways. Every day brings new apps, updates, and challenges that require constant adaptation. Kathy embraces this dynamic space, seeing it as an opportunity to learn, grow, and share her experiences—both successes and missteps—with others.

Social media has opened doors for direct audience engagement, allowing creators to build lasting relationships with their followers. However, it also presents challenges, including concerns over mental health, misinformation, and privacy. Kathy acknowledges the need for balance and mindful usage, ensuring that her content remains authentic, valuable, and uplifting.

Building a Connection with the Audience

One of Kathy's greatest strengths is her ability to connect with her audience. She attributes this to her genuine passion for sharing what she loves in an engaging and entertaining way. Creating content that resonates with people requires a deep understanding of their needs and interests. Kathy values audience feedback, using it as a guide to refine her content and ensure she is providing value.

Her approach involves defining her target audience, identifying their challenges, and crafting messages that speak to them on an emotional level. This connection is at the heart of her success as a lifestyle creator and TV host.

Looking to the Future

Kathy's dream of working with a wellness-inspired, worldwide luxury hotel brand that offers unique and exceptional services has come true! She is thrilled to be the ambassador for Corbo Collection, a portfolio of luxury hotels around the globe that she is excited to share with her audience. This opportunity allows her to merge her love for lifestyle content with luxury travel, bringing her followers exclusive insights into some of the most exquisite destinations in the world.

Beyond this, Kathy continues to collaborate with top brands such as Garcia de la Cruz, Sony, Nissan, and Laura Geller Beauty and local hotels such as The Godfrey and London Hotel, among many others. She considers these partnerships a true blessing, allowing her to connect with brands she genuinely loves and trusts.

As she looks ahead, Kathy remains committed to expanding her audience, working with brands that align with her values, and sharing her passions through her television segments. Her advice to others? The world is vast, and there is always space for you. If you find yourself in a place where you don't fit, close that door and move forward. The universe wants you to succeed—embrace that truth, and you will thrive.

A Legacy of Passion and Purpose

Kathy Copcutt's journey is a powerful reminder that success is not a linear path but a series of unexpected turns that lead to incredible opportunities. By staying open, adaptable, and passionate about her work, she has built a career that is both fulfilling and impactful. Whether on television, at the Emmys, or connecting with her audience online, Kathy continues to inspire, uplift, and leave a lasting mark in the media industry.

CONNECT WITH KATHY

www.livewithkathy.com
Instagram: @livewithkathy

EVERYTHING IS WITHIN YOUR POWER, AND YOUR POWER IS WITHIN YOU.

Women's History Month

COCO CHANEL:
THE WOMAN WHO REVOLUTIONIZED FASHION

Coco Chanel didn't just design clothes—she rewrote the rules of fashion. At a time when women were bound by corsets and elaborate dresses, she introduced a new vision: elegance with freedom, simplicity with sophistication. With her bold ideas and unshakable determination, Chanel not only became one of the most influential designers in history but also an enduring symbol of independence and reinvention.

Born Gabrielle Bonheur Chanel in 1883 in Saumur, France, her early life was far from glamorous. After the death of her mother, young Gabrielle was sent to an orphanage, where she learned the art of sewing from the nuns who raised her. Though the convent was strict, it unknowingly shaped her destiny, instilling in her the skills that would later revolutionize fashion.

As a young woman, she tried her hand at singing in cafés, where she earned the nickname *"Coco."* Though music wasn't her calling, she developed a taste for luxury and ambition, qualities that led her to Paris—the city where she would build her empire.

Chanel's first step into fashion came with a small hat shop in 1910, funded by a wealthy admirer. Her designs were unlike anything seen before: sleek, simple, and free from excess. Her hats became a sensation, drawing the attention of Parisian high society. But she wasn't content with just accessories—she wanted to change the way women dressed.

By the 1920s, Chanel had done just that. She introduced jersey fabric, traditionally used for men's underwear, and turned it into chic, wearable fashion. She created the little black dress—an effortlessly elegant piece that became a staple in every woman's wardrobe. She made trousers fashionable for women, proving that style could be both feminine and practical.

Perhaps her greatest invention was Chanel No. 5, the world's first designer fragrance. Unlike the floral, delicate perfumes of the time, it was bold, complex, and unforgettable—just like the woman who created it.

Her influence extended far beyond clothing. Chanel embodied a new kind of woman—one who was confident, independent, and unapologetically herself. She rejected the idea that women should dress for men, instead designing for the modern woman who lived, worked, and moved with freedom.

Her empire grew, but so did the challenges. During World War II, Chanel closed her boutiques and faced controversy over her associations during the Nazi occupation of France. For a time, it seemed her legacy might fade. But in 1954, at the age of 71, she made an extraordinary comeback, reintroducing the Chanel suit—an iconic look that would be worn by powerful women for generations, from Jackie Kennedy to Princess Diana.

Coco Chanel passed away in 1971, but her impact remains undeniable. Her brand continues to define luxury, her designs still shape fashion, and her fearless spirit inspires women worldwide. She proved that style is more than fabric—it's an attitude, a revolution, and a legacy that never fades.

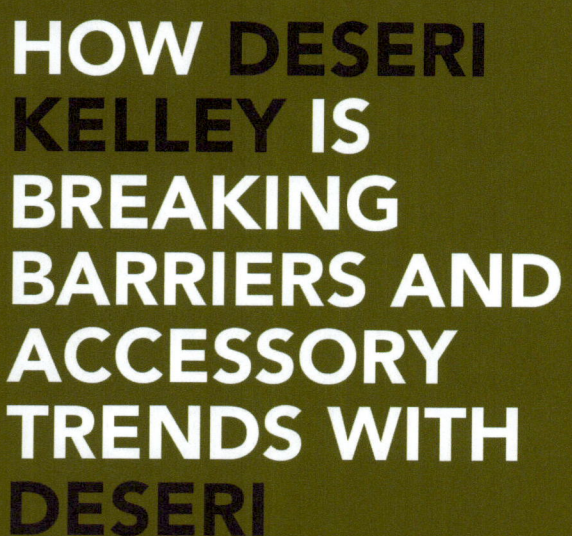

HOW DESERI KELLEY IS BREAKING BARRIERS AND ACCESSORY TRENDS WITH DESERI

To start things off...I'm Deseri Kelley, the founder and designer behind DESERI, a luxury handbag brand based in Texas. DESERI is all about timeless elegance with a bold, modern edge, crafted for women who appreciate high-quality craftsmanship and statement-making designs. I created DESERI because I believe handbags should be more than just accessories; they should be pieces of art that empower the women who carry them. Our brand is rooted in luxury but also in accessibility, giving women pieces that make them feel confident, stylish, and unstoppable.

Beyond fashion, I'm a wife and a proud mom to two incredible sons. Family is everything to me, and my journey as a wife and mother has deeply influenced my perspective on business and creativity. Before launching DESERI, my career was in education and I had the life-changing experience of living overseas in Spain and France. Those experiences shaped my appreciation for global fashion, culture, and craftsmanship; elements that continue to inspire the brand today.

When it comes to inspirational fashion icons, there are so many, but a few that come to mind are Miuccia Prada, Gabriela Hearst, and Rihanna. Miuccia Prada has an incredible ability to merge intellect with fashion, making statements that go beyond aesthetics. Gabriela Hearst is redefining luxury with sustainability, which I deeply respect. And Rihanna, she's fearless. She's built a brand that refuses to conform, and that level of authenticity is something I admire and strive for with DESERI. Each of these women has influenced the industry by pushing boundaries, challenging norms, and showing that fashion can be both powerful and purposeful.

DESERI is breaking barriers in a few ways. First, as a Black-owned luxury brand, I'm committed to showing that high fashion and luxury aren't limited to European heritage houses. Representation in this space matters, and I want DESERI to be part of that shift. Secondly, I'm focused on redefining what modern luxury looks like, it's not just about exclusivity but about impact. We are working towards expanding our product range while maintaining impeccable craftsmanship, making sure luxury is both aspirational and attainable.

I'm really proud of our upcoming Spring 2025 collection. We're elevating our designs while staying true to our signature aesthetic, and we're capturing some incredible behind-the-scenes content to bring our audience deeper into the world of DESERI. I've also been working on expanding into boutiques and department stores, ensuring our bags are available to a wider audience. Looking ahead, we're exploring new product categories, think luxury beyond handbags. The vision is big, and I can't wait to bring it all to life.

In fashion, I think we're moving toward a more intentional fashion space. Consumers are looking for brands with real stories, real craftsmanship, and real values. I see a shift towards quiet luxury, but not in the traditional sense; more about thoughtful design and longevity rather than just minimalism. I also think technology will continue to play a big role, whether through AI-driven design, sustainable innovations, or even how brands connect with their customers. At DESERI, we're watching these shifts closely and making sure we stay ahead while staying true to our DNA.

CONNECT WITH DESERI

www.deseri.com
www.instagram.com/deseriofficial

JOSEPHINE BAKER:
THE DANCER WHO DEFIED BOUNDARIES

Josephine Baker was more than just a performer—she was a force of nature. As a trailblazing entertainer, a fearless activist, and a symbol of unapologetic self-expression, Baker captivated audiences while shattering racial and societal barriers. Her life was a masterpiece of reinvention, resilience, and resistance, making her one of the most influential women of the 20th century.

Born in 1906 in St. Louis, Missouri, Baker grew up in a segregated America, where opportunities for Black performers were severely limited. Poverty and racial discrimination shaped her early years, but she found solace in dance. By the age of 15, she had joined a vaudeville troupe, using her talent and charm to escape the harsh realities of her upbringing. When the racial climate in the U.S. proved suffocating, she set her sights on France—a country that would embrace her like no other.

Baker arrived in Paris in 1925 and instantly became the city's most electrifying performer. With her daring costumes, uninhibited performances, and magnetic presence, she revolutionized entertainment. Her famed *"banana skirt"* dance at the Folies Bergère was both provocative and groundbreaking, challenging Western ideals of beauty and sensuality. Paris fell in love with her, and she became the highest-paid entertainer in Europe, a remarkable feat for a Black woman in that era.

Beyond her entertainment career, Baker used her fame as a tool for activism. During World War II, she worked as a spy for the French Resistance, using her performances as cover while smuggling intelligence for the Allies. With coded messages hidden in sheet music and her ability to travel freely, she risked her life to fight against fascism. Her courage earned her the Croix de Guerre and the Legion of Honor, two of France's highest military distinctions.

Baker's activism extended beyond wartime efforts. As the Civil Rights Movement gained momentum in the U.S., she refused to perform for segregated audiences, challenging the very institutions that once rejected her. In 1963, she stood alongside Martin Luther King Jr. at the March on Washington, the only woman to give a speech that day. Clad in her Free French uniform and medals, she spoke passionately about racial justice, urging America to live up to its ideals of equality and freedom.

Her commitment to a more just world also extended to her personal life. She adopted 12 children from different racial and cultural backgrounds, calling them her *"Rainbow Tribe."* She believed in a world without prejudice and raised her children to embody that vision. Her home in France became a symbol of unity, a living testament to her belief that humanity could overcome divisions.

Josephine Baker remained an icon until her final days. In 1975, she returned to the stage for a comeback performance in Paris. Just days later, she passed away at 68, leaving behind a legacy that transcended entertainment. She had danced, sung, and fought her way into history, proving that art and activism could coexist powerfully.

In 2021, France honored her by inducting her into the Panthéon, the country's highest posthumous recognition—a tribute reserved for national heroes. She was the first Black woman to receive this honor, a testament to her lasting impact.

Josephine Baker was more than a performer; she was a movement. She redefined beauty, fought for justice, and inspired generations to break free from limitations. She proved that a woman could be both dazzling and defiant, an artist and an activist, a dreamer and a fighter. Her story is one of triumph against all odds—a reminder that true greatness knows no boundaries.

SUSIE CRINER:
HOUSTON'S MUSIC MAVEN

In 1979, Susie Criner founded and began operating Houston's iconic live music venue, Rockefeller's, which hosted some of the greatest musicians of the time (and of all time), like Ray Charles, Ella Fitzgerald, James Brown, B.B. King, Dave Matthews Band, Garth Brooks, The Chicks (formerly The Dixie Chicks), The Pointer Sisters, The Fabulous Thunderbirds, Etta James, Lyle Lovett, and many more.

Can you imagine a better celebrity performer line up than that?
As Susie tells it, one night, a guest approached her at The Four Tops show at Rockefeller's, asking if he could book them for his daughter's debutante ball, a private event.

That question was an *"ah ha"* moment for Susie, who took the opportunity to become an agent for individuals looking for help with a celebrity booking. So Susie started her own private and corporate entertainment booking agency, now called Gulf Coast Entertainment.

For 45 years, GCE has distinguished itself in the market by representing the buyer of entertainment with talent booking for private performances across the country, rather than representing the artist. Though of course, as you will read here, supporting art and artists has always been incredibly important to Susie.

GCE specializes in corporate event entertainment in booking celebrity talent such as a celebrity speaker, headliner, musician, artist, talent, actor, entertainer, or other celebrity performer for a special event, wedding, or brand campaign.

Over the years, Gulf Coast Entertainment has helped its clients hire hundreds of celebrity entertainers for an appearance or performance at private and social events throughout the country, and has served as the talent agency for hundreds of Fortune 500 companies in Houston and beyond.

From celebrity talent like Lionel Richie to a public figure and actor like Jerry Seinfeld, Gulf Coast Entertainment has been the go-to celebrity booking service for booking quality entertainment for private performances for 45 years.

Susie has established strong ties with high-end event professionals and clients throughout the country over the years, and has a reputation for being a booking agent that produces the highest quality entertainment, while making the event seamless for the client and artist.

Whether an event planner approaches her to help with the booking process to hire a celebrity performer for an appearance at a corporate event, or a client wants the best party band to perform for a high-end wedding reception, Susie relishes the opportunity to help her clients find the perfect talent for their private event.

A Charter Member of the Rock & Roll Hall of Fame, Susie is a luminary in the music world, known for her booking agency brand Gulf Coast Entertainment. She has also been honored by many initiatives in Houston for her philanthropic efforts as well, the Contemporary Arts Museum, Houston, for which she served as a Board member for many years, and Hermann Park Conservancy.

Susie's work in support of the arts, green space, and other philanthropic efforts in Houston is stunning. She served for years as a Board Member of the Contemporary Arts Museum Houston, Diverse Works, The Orange Show, the Museum of Fine Arts Houston, The Menil Collection, and Rice Design Alliance, among many others. Susie has dedicated her life to supporting her community, the arts, and entertainment, both through her philanthropic work and her professional life.

Susie is a trusted resource in booking celebrity talent. She loves working with event professionals and helping clients find the perfect talent to meet their special event needs. Making sure the entertainer aligns with the event planner's and client's brand and goals is of utmost importance to Susie. She tailors the booking process to make sure the talent agency finds the perfect entertainer to hire, whether it be a public figure, celebrity chef, artist, celebrity speaker, actor, or celebrity talent like Shania Twain or John Legend!

Talent booking is made simple by working with Susie and her agency, Gulf Coast Entertainment. They can help with talent booking of all kinds, not only with a celebrity booking for a private event or speaking engagement, but also a party band booking for private performances and weddings.

Whether you're working with an event planner or booking your corporate entertainment on your own, GCE serves as your agent and represents You in the process of working with a talent agency to find the perfect talent for your event.

45 years after Susie founded Rockefeller's, she still loves music as much as she always has and enjoys providing her celebrity booking agency service to event professionals, event planners, and individuals with their corporate entertainment.

Susie is known for considering every detail as your dedicated booking agent for your special event. Having her in your corner, you know the booking process will be seamless. Booking a celebrity speaker, public figure, or entertainer for an appearance has never been easier with Gulf Coast Entertainment as your personal celebrity booking agency!

CONNECT WITH SUSIE

www.instagram.com/gulfcoastentertainment
www.facebook.com/GCEntertain
www.linkedin.com/company/gulf-coast-entertainment
www.gulfcoastentertainment.com

CELIA CRUZ:
THE QUEEN WHO MADE THE WORLD DANCE

Celia Cruz was more than just a singer—she was a force of nature. With her electrifying stage presence, dazzling costumes, and a voice that could ignite a room, she became the undisputed *"Queen of Salsa."* Over a career spanning more than five decades, Cruz not only redefined Latin music but also became a symbol of resilience, passion, and the unbreakable spirit of her Cuban heritage.

Born Úrsula Hilaria Celia de la Caridad Cruz Alfonso in Havana, Cuba, in 1925, Celia grew up surrounded by the rhythms of Afro-Cuban music. Her father wanted her to become a teacher, but music was her true calling. She started singing in school, and by her teenage years, she was winning local contests and radio competitions. Her powerful voice, rich with emotion and energy, set her apart early on, but she had no idea that she was destined for global stardom.

Celia's big break came in 1950 when she became the lead singer of La Sonora Matancera, Cuba's most famous band at the time. With her at the helm, the group became a sensation across Latin America, filling dance floors from Havana to Mexico City. Her voice carried the heartbeat of Cuba, and she infused every performance with joy, improvisation, and her signature call—*"¡Azúcar!"*—a word that became synonymous with her infectious energy.

In 1960, as Fidel Castro rose to power, Celia and her band traveled to Mexico for a performance. She made a life-changing decision: she would not return to Cuba. The government soon banned her music, labeling her a traitor, but she refused to let politics silence her. Instead, she took her talent to the United States, where she became a key figure in New York City's burgeoning salsa movement.

While many assumed her career might suffer in exile, Celia Cruz only grew stronger. She collaborated with legendary musicians like Tito Puente, Willie Colón, and Johnny Pacheco, fusing traditional Cuban sounds with modern salsa. Her influence helped push Latin music onto the world stage, making salsa not just a genre but a movement.

Her performances were nothing short of magical. With extravagant sequined gowns, towering wigs, and boundless energy, she captivated audiences everywhere. But it wasn't just her style that made her a star—it was her presence. She sang about love, culture, and resilience, giving a voice to the millions of immigrants who carried their heritage with pride.

Over the years, she released more than 70 albums, earned multiple Grammy and Latin Grammy Awards, and performed for sold-out crowds across the world. Yet, through all the fame and accolades, she remained deeply connected to her roots. She never returned to Cuba, but her music kept the island alive in her heart.

Celia Cruz's final years were as grand as her career. Even after being diagnosed with brain cancer in 2002, she continued to record, determined to leave behind a legacy that would outlive her. She passed away in 2003, but her influence never faded. Today, her songs are still played at celebrations, inspiring new generations to dance, dream, and embrace their heritage with pride.

In 2016, the Smithsonian honored her with a special exhibit, and in 2023, she became the first Afro-Latina to appear on a U.S. quarter, a fitting tribute to a woman who shattered barriers and defined a genre.

Celia Cruz didn't just sing—she transformed music. She made the world dance, and in doing so, she proved that passion, resilience, and a love for one's culture can create a legacy that echoes for generations. She will always be la Reina, the Queen of Salsa, whose voice and spirit will never fade. ¡Azúcar!

www.sherisesstudios.com

she wins
Women's Network

Empowering Women Entrepreneurs to Thrive Locally and Globally

Transform your life and business with access to exclusive resources, strategic networking, and unwavering support.

Benefits:
➤ *Strategic networking & mentorship*
➤ *Masterclasses & exclusive resources*
➤ *Member spotlights & VIP perks*

Join for just
$87/MONTH
no contracts, cancel anytime.

Start thriving today. Join She Wins Women's Network!

www.shewinswomensnetwork.com

HOW GITHA DUNCKER IS BREAKING NORMS IN SWIM AND READY TO WEAR WITH AQUARI

To start things off...Aquari is a contemporary swimwear and lifestyle brand that blends style, comfort, and sustainability. Our collections feature easy-to-wear, travel-ready essentials designed for the modern explorer. We're committed to using eco-friendly fabrics, maintaining ethical practices throughout our supply chain, and partnering with charitable initiatives. At Aquari, we believe fashion can be both conscious in design and spirit. Inspired by the Age of Aquarius, we envision a future where fashion serves as a catalyst for positive change. Founded in Austin, Designed in Los Angeles, Made in the U.S.A.

As the fashion industry experiences a collective awakening towards eco-consciousness, I am deeply inspired by the women and brands who have paved the way for years. Stella McCartney has always led the charge in sustainable fashion, while Coco Chanel single-handedly revolutionized women's clothing. Diane von Furstenberg empowered women with both style and confidence. These trailblazing women have not only shaped the industry but also inspired a movement toward more conscious and impactful fashion.

At Aquari, sustainability is not just a trend—it's a way of life. We are dedicated to sparking a shift towards conscious consumerism by creating products that are made to be cherished and enjoyed for years, not discarded after a season. Our mission is to design with intention, prioritizing durability, timelessness, and eco-friendly practices in every piece. We believe in a future where fashion isn't just about style, but about making choices that contribute to a healthier planet. By focusing on quality and sustainability, we aim to inspire our customers to invest in pieces that reflect both their values and their love for lasting design, fostering a connection that extends beyond the product to a shared commitment to a more sustainable future.

Recently, we've been focusing on enhancing our sustainability efforts, including sourcing eco-friendly materials and maintaining ethical standards throughout our supply chain. We're particularly proud of our partnerships with Los Angeles-based manufacturers who share our values of fair labor practices and ethical working conditions. Additionally, we've been refining our eco-friendly packaging and shipping methods to reduce our environmental impact further.

Another project we're excited about is our charitable initiative, Eden People + Planet. Through this, we actively contribute to tree planting and global reforestation efforts, helping to restore the environment. Looking ahead, we're committed to continuing our work on minimizing waste with innovative techniques and further reducing our carbon footprint. Our ultimate goal is to lead the way in conscious consumerism, fostering a more sustainable and eco-conscious future for fashion.

In the coming years, I see fashion moving towards greater sustainability and inclusivity. Eco-friendly materials and circular fashion practices will become more mainstream, with brands prioritizing recycled, upcycled, and biodegradable fabrics. Transparency will also grow, with consumers demanding more insight into supply chains and product impacts.

Inclusivity will remain key, with a focus on diversity in size, gender, and culture. Fashion will empower everyone to express themselves authentically, celebrating individuality.

Ultimately, I expect a shift toward conscious consumerism, where style and ethics go hand in hand, leading to positive, lasting change in the industry.

CONNECT WITH GITHA

www.theaquari.com
www.instagram.com/theaquari

MARILYN MONROE:
THE TIMELESS ICON WHO REDEFINED STARDOM

Few figures in history have captivated the world quite like Marilyn Monroe. More than just a Hollywood starlet, she was a cultural phenomenon, a woman whose beauty, charisma, and vulnerability made her unforgettable. Decades after her passing, Monroe remains a symbol of glamour, strength, and mystery. But beyond the dazzling image was a woman of intelligence, ambition, and depth—one who fought to control her own narrative in an industry that often sought to define her.

Born Norma Jeane Mortenson in 1926, Marilyn Monroe's early life was far from the glitz and glamour she would later embody. Raised in foster homes and orphanages, she endured an unstable childhood marked by hardship. However, Monroe's resilience never wavered. She found solace in movies, dreaming of a life beyond the limitations imposed on her.

Her journey to stardom began when she was discovered as a model, leading to her first film contracts in the late 1940s. Hollywood executives quickly recognized her magnetic appeal, but she was often typecast as the *"dumb blonde"* in comedies and musical films. Despite the limitations placed upon her, Monroe's intelligence and determination pushed her to seek more substantial roles. She took acting classes, studied her craft, and eventually proved herself as more than just a pretty face.

By the 1950s, Monroe had become the world's most famous woman. Films like Gentlemen Prefer Blondes (1953), How to Marry a Millionaire (1953), and The Seven Year Itch (1955) solidified her as a box-office sensation.

Her blend of innocence and sensuality made her irresistible to audiences, but Monroe longed for respect as an actress. In pursuit of artistic credibility, she moved to New York and studied under the legendary Lee Strasberg at the Actors Studio. This dedication led to one of her most acclaimed performances in Bus Stop (1956), proving she had the talent to match her star power.

However, Monroe's rise to fame came at a cost. The pressures of stardom, personal struggles, and a relentless media spotlight took their toll. Yet, even in her most difficult moments, she remained a force to be reckoned with. She founded her own production company—a revolutionary move for a woman in Hollywood at the time—and continued to challenge the industry's expectations of her.

Beyond the screen, Monroe was deeply passionate about social issues. She used her influence to advocate for racial equality, famously ensuring that jazz singer Ella Fitzgerald was given a stage at the Mocambo nightclub. Her personal life was filled with complexities, from her high-profile marriages to Joe DiMaggio and Arthur Miller to her struggles with mental health. Yet, her resilience and humanity made her all the more compelling.

Monroe's tragic death at the age of 36 in 1962 shocked the world, but her legacy endures. Her impact on pop culture remains unparalleled— her image continues to inspire fashion, art, and film. She was more than a sex symbol; she was a woman ahead of her time, unafraid to chase her dreams despite the odds. Marilyn Monroe was, and always will be, the ultimate icon of Hollywood's golden age.

HOW NOA ARIAS AND SHAULA YEMINI ARE BREAKING NORMS IN THE LINGERIE INDUSTRY WITH BLOOMERS INTIMATES

To start things off...We are a mother-daughter team on a mission to make sexy and comfortable lingerie for women of all ages, shapes and sizes. Our bodies change over time, for example after having a baby, or gaining a few pounds or a few years and we now crave more comfort and support than before. And, while we don't want to be relegated to cotton granny panties or suffer thongs, we still want to look and feel great in our lingerie. That's where Bloomers Intimates come in! Our full coverage, high waisted styles offer all the support, comfort and coverage women crave, while still keeping them true to their sexiest selves.

In terms of inspiration, Coco Chanel is truly a visionary. She revolutionized women's fashion by introducing timeless pieces like the little black dress and the power suit, not to mention luxury handbags. And her designs are still fashionable to this day! We are inspired by Donna Karan for her sophisticated yet classic, and practical designs that empower women to feel confident and chic in their everyday lives (which is something we aspire to at Bloomers). Josie Natori, who basically transformed luxury loungewear and lingerie into high fashion. These women not only transformed the industry but have also provided women with new ways to feel confident, empowered and chic every day.

Before Bloomers Intimates came about, the standard for comfort had been big cotton granny panties. Granny panties, while super comfortable, are not very attractive and usually cause terrible visible panty lines. And, on the opposite end of the lingerie spectrum, you have thongs, which are the epitome of sexy but also a literal pain in the rear. We set out to combine the comfort of granny panties with the sexy allure of lace, to produce undies that are as stylish as they are comfortable. Our designs use soft 4-way stretch lace to create full coverage panties that stay put and eliminate panty lines, combining the advantages of both styles.

We've recently worked hand in hand with a top lace manufacturer to create lace that is soft as a feather, strong, and super stretchy - naturally we call it Feather Lace. It took a long time to develop, but it was worth it! We just launched Her Highness Briefs and Pantyloon® Slip Shorts in Feather Lace, and will extend it to other styles in the near future. We are also very proud of another industry first: our lace SneezeProof undies. These are the only sexy leakproof underwear styles on the market. Our SneezeProof undies absorb up to 1 teaspoon of liquid for those *"oops"* moments while exercising, sneezing or coughing, or after giving birth when your pelvic floor muscles are weaker.

We expect to see more products combining function and style for women of all ages in the future. For years, the emphasis was on style for the young and the thin - gorgeous products for young women with perfect bodies. But as you grow older, and your body changes, so do your lingerie needs. In the past, most lingerie didn't fit, didn't flatter, and didn't meet your needs but now there is a new emphasis on inclusivity. Inclusivity will continue to be a focus for all ages, shapes, sizes, and accessibility for women of varying abilities. Function will also continue to be a focus including active and sports styles as well as leakproof.

CONNECT WITH NOA & SHAULA

www.bloomersintimates.com
www.instagram.com/bloomersintimates

DOLLY PARTON:
THE VOICE, THE VISION, THE LEGEND

Dolly Parton is more than just a country music legend—she is an unstoppable force of creativity, kindness, and resilience. With a voice that can move mountains and a heart that gives endlessly, she has spent decades breaking barriers, redefining success, and inspiring generations. From humble beginnings in the hills of Tennessee to international superstardom, Dolly's story is one of grit, grace, and generosity.

Born in 1946 in Locust Ridge, Tennessee, Dolly Rebecca Parton was one of twelve children in a family that struggled to make ends meet. Music was always in her soul, and she started singing in church before taking her talents to local radio stations. By the age of 13, she had recorded her first song and performed at the Grand Ole Opry. But Dolly wasn't just another young singer with a dream—she had a vision, and she was determined to make it a reality.

After high school, she moved to Nashville, the heart of country music, and quickly made a name for herself as a songwriter. Her big break came when she was invited to join The Porter Wagoner Show in 1967, a move that introduced her to a national audience. Before long, she had established herself as a solo artist, releasing hit after hit. Songs like Jolene, Coat of Many Colors, and I Will Always Love You became instant classics, showcasing not just her powerful voice but her exceptional songwriting ability.

Dolly's music is deeply personal, often reflecting her own struggles and triumphs. Coat of Many Colors, for example, tells the story of a childhood wrapped in love rather than wealth. I Will Always Love You, written as a farewell to Porter Wagoner, later became a global sensation when Whitney Houston recorded it for The Bodyguard soundtrack.

But Dolly Parton is not just a musician—she is an empire. She built Dollywood, a theme park that celebrates her roots and provides jobs for thousands. She launched businesses, created her own record label, and became one of the most influential women in entertainment. Yet, despite her immense success, she never lost touch with where she came from.

Her philanthropy is as legendary as her music. Through the Dollywood Foundation, she has championed literacy, creating the Imagination Library, which has gifted millions of books to children worldwide. She has also supported disaster relief, healthcare initiatives, and education programs, all with the same warmth and authenticity that define her music.

Dolly has never let anyone define her. With her signature rhinestones and sky-high wigs, she embraces her larger-than-life persona while remaining one of the most down-to-earth celebrities. She is a symbol of perseverance, proving that a young girl from the Smoky Mountains could rise to become one of the most beloved and influential women in history.

Even after decades in the spotlight, Dolly Parton continues to inspire. Whether through her music, her philanthropy, or her unwavering belief in kindness and hard work, she remains a true icon—a living legend who has not only shaped country music but the world itself.

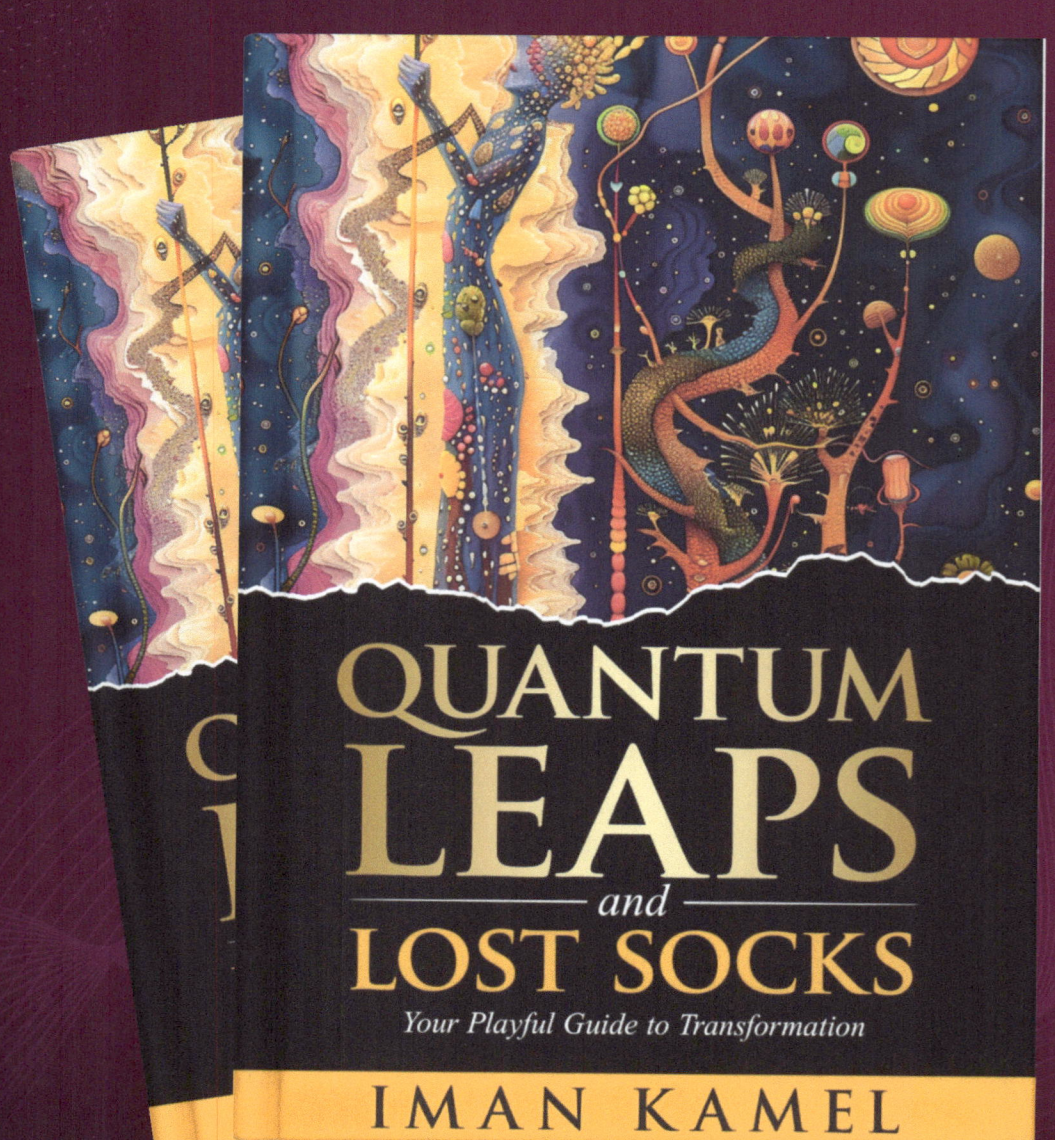

HOW TRACY VONTÉLLE GREEN AND NANCEY FLOWERS-HARRIS ARE BREAKING BARRIERS WITH VONTÉLLE

To start things off...We are Nancey and Tracy, the proud creators of Vontélle Eyewear. Vontélle was born out of a personal need—finding stylish eyewear that fits well for those of us with unique facial features, like wider nose bridges and higher cheekbones. We quickly realized that many others were facing the same challenge, so we set out to create a solution.

Vontélle is more than just an eyewear brand; we specialize in offering glasses that cater to diverse facial features, ensuring a comfortable and stylish fit for everyone. Our mission is to provide eyewear that makes people feel confident, represented, and seen, while also celebrating diversity in design. Our frames are not only fashionable but also functional, designed with high-quality materials and attention to detail. We pride ourselves on offering eyewear that suits a wide range of face shapes and sizes, empowering people to express their individuality.

We're passionate about making a difference in the eyewear industry, and we're excited to continue growing Vontélle while bringing comfort, style, and representation to the forefront.

Some women who inspire us in the fashion industry are Bethann Hardison, Iris Apfel, Donna Karan, and Ann Cole Lowe. Bethann Hardison has been a trailblazer for diversity and inclusion, advocating for greater representation of people of color in fashion. Iris Apfel's bold, eclectic style teaches us to embrace individuality and creativity, showing that fashion is about expressing personality at any age. Donna Karan revolutionized fashion with her *"7 easy pieces"* philosophy, combining modern elegance with practicality, influencing how women approach functional yet stylish clothing. Ann Cole Lowe, one of the first African-American women to succeed in couture design, broke barriers and paved the way for women of color in high fashion. These women shape how we approach style, inclusivity, and self-expression.

At Vontélle, we are committed to fostering variety and representation in every aspect of our business. Our focus is on creating eyewear that caters to a broad spectrum of facial features, cultures, and identities, ensuring that everyone can find a style that reflects their unique personality and needs. Through our designs and brand ethos, we aim to highlight the beauty of individuality and ensure that all customers feel valued and seen.

In addition, we embrace different cultures and identities in everything we do, from our designs to our brand message. Vontélle is dedicated to ensuring our frames reflect the beauty of individuality and personal expression. We are also working to increase visibility in the fashion and eyewear industries, empowering those who have traditionally been overlooked.

Through our commitment to inclusivity, exceptional design, and functionality, Vontélle is helping reshape the eyewear industry, making it more accessible and welcoming to everyone, regardless of their face shape or background.

We are incredibly pleased with the America's Best project we did in 2024 and are honored to have been presented with the Distinctive Design Award from the National Vision Council. This achievement means a lot to us, and we are proud to be recognized for our efforts to bring inclusivity and style to the eyewear industry.

We're also thrilled about our collaborations with actor and philanthropist Kadeem Hardison, as well as renowned illustrator Kendra Dandy.

These partnerships have helped elevate the Vontélle brand and reinforce our mission to offer eyewear that celebrates individuality and diversity.

Looking ahead, we have an exciting upcoming partnership with a celebrated 20th-century artist, which will bring new and unique designs to our collections. Additionally, we're planning to introduce beautiful new styles in the second half of 2025 that will further expand our product offerings and continue to reflect our commitment to inclusivity and high-quality design.

We're excited about the future and the continued growth of Vontélle as we work to reshape the eyewear industry and create even more opportunities for individuals to express themselves through style.

In the coming years, we see fashion evolving with a stronger emphasis on sustainability, inclusivity, and technology. As consumers become more aware of the environmental impact of their purchases, the industry will shift toward eco-friendly materials and transparent production processes. Inclusivity will also continue to grow, with more brands embracing size diversity, gender-neutral options, and designs that cater to various body types, face shapes, and cultural identities.

The industry will break traditional norms, creating space for all forms of self-expression. Technology will play a larger role, from virtual try-ons to smart fabrics that enhance the wearer's experience. Ultimately, fashion will focus more on individuality and self-expression, moving away from fast trends to designs that resonate with personal values. It's an exciting time for the industry.

CONNECT WITH TRACY & NANCEY

www.vontelle.com
www.instagram.com/vontelleeyewear

LAVERNE COX:
REDEFINING REPRESENTATION, BREAKING BARRIERS

But Laverne Cox's impact extends far beyond the screen. She has used her platform to advocate for transgender rights, visibility, and equality. Her speeches, interviews, and public appearances consistently emphasize the need for inclusivity and understanding. She has spoken at the White House, marched for justice, and challenged lawmakers to create policies that protect transgender individuals from discrimination and violence.

Fashion and beauty industries have also taken note of Cox's influence. She became the first openly transgender person to grace the cover of TIME magazine in 2014, with the powerful headline, The Transgender Tipping Point. Since then, she has appeared on covers of Vogue, Cosmopolitan, and other major publications, proving that beauty exists in all forms. As a model, she has walked prestigious runways, further cementing her place as a cultural icon.

Her work in entertainment continues to break new ground. Cox has starred in critically acclaimed films, narrated documentaries about transgender experiences, and produced content that elevates marginalized voices. She made history again as the first openly transgender person to have a Barbie doll modeled after her—a milestone in representation that she hopes will inspire young people to embrace their authenticity.

Despite her success, Cox remains deeply connected to her mission. She reminds the world that visibility is not just about being seen—it's about being understood, respected, and valued. She champions policies that protect trans youth, fights against discrimination, and uplifts voices that have long been silenced.

Laverne Cox is not just a Hollywood star; she is a movement. Her courage, talent, and unwavering dedication to equality make her one of the most influential figures of our time. In every role she plays—on-screen and off—she reminds us all of the power of living boldly, unapologetically, and authentically.

Laverne Cox is a name that resonates far beyond Hollywood. She is more than an actress—she is a trailblazer, an advocate, and a symbol of empowerment for marginalized communities. As the first openly transgender person nominated for a Primetime Emmy and a force for representation in media, Cox has shattered glass ceilings while redefining beauty, talent, and visibility in entertainment.

Born in Mobile, Alabama, in 1972, Laverne Cox's early years were marked by struggle and self-discovery. Growing up in the South as a transgender woman of color was not easy, but Cox found solace in the arts. She pursued dance, acting, and performance, earning a degree from Marymount Manhattan College. It was in New York City that she began her journey toward becoming a voice for the underrepresented.

Cox's breakthrough came when she was cast as Sophia Burset on Netflix's Orange Is the New Black in 2013. Her portrayal of Sophia, a transgender inmate navigating both the prison system and her personal identity, was groundbreaking. For the first time, audiences saw a trans woman playing a trans character with nuance and depth—something rarely, if ever, seen in mainstream television. The role earned Cox an Emmy nomination, making her the first openly transgender person to receive such an honor.

www.sherisesstudios.com

FENIX TV

YOUR PLATFORM, YOUR VOICE, YOUR POWER!

Step into the Spotlight as a Host on FENIX TV!

Are you ready to amplify your message, inspire others, and be part of a groundbreaking network dedicated to **empowering women worldwide**? FENIX TV is your platform to **shine as a host**, share your expertise, and connect with a global audience.

WHY HOST ON FENIX TV?

- Reach a worldwide audience passionate about empowerment
- Showcase your voice, brand, and expertise
- Join a community of inspiring leaders and changemakers
- Be part of a network that uplifts and celebrates women

Whether you dream of leading a talk show, sharing powerful stories, or educating and inspiring others—FENIX TV is where your voice matters!

SPOTS ARE LIMITED! Secure your hosting opportunity today.

 Contact us now at
info@fenixtv.app

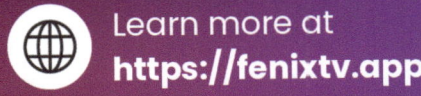 Learn more at
https://fenixtv.app

THE POWER TO REBUILD:
HOW CHRISTINA JOHNSON TURNED ADVERSITY INTO VICTORY

Christina Johnson's story is one of resilience, determination, and transformation. From becoming a mother as a teenager to building multiple successful businesses, overcoming personal trauma, and facing significant health challenges, she has continually defied expectations and forged a path of empowerment. Her journey is a testament to the power of self-belief, perseverance, and the willingness to rewrite one's own narrative.

Becoming a mother as a teenager often comes with societal expectations of struggle, dependence, and unfulfilled potential. However, Christina refused to let circumstances dictate her future. She embraced motherhood with fierce determination, choosing to rise above the challenges and create a life defined by strength and ambition. Rather than succumbing to the limitations often placed on young mothers, she pursued personal and professional growth with relentless dedication.

Her entrepreneurial spirit led her to establish multiple businesses, demonstrating her keen ability to navigate the complexities of leadership and innovation. Entrepreneurship was not just a career path for Christina—it was a way to reclaim control over her life, to build something meaningful not only for herself but for those she sought to inspire. Through her ventures, she proved that success is not reserved for those with conventional beginnings but is available to those who dare to dream beyond their circumstances.

In addition to her professional accomplishments, Christina has been deeply committed to personal development and self-healing. Having faced significant trauma, she chose to confront her past with courage and grace, embarking on a journey of self-discovery and transformation. She recognized that healing was not a destination but a continuous process of self-reflection, faith, and intentional growth.

Her faith has been an anchor throughout her journey. Rather than viewing her struggles as setbacks, she has seen them as opportunities for deepening her relationship with God. Through scripture, prayer, and unwavering belief, she has found solace and strength, turning even the darkest moments into lessons of resilience. Her ability to find purpose in pain has allowed her to connect with others on a profound level, offering hope and encouragement to those who may be walking similar paths.

One of the most transformative periods of Christina's life began in 2009 when she was diagnosed with Graves' disease, an autoimmune disorder that commonly affects the thyroid gland. This diagnosis set her on a journey of deep self-reflection, resilience, and healing.

Over the course of several years, she underwent three surgeries, each one challenging her physically, emotionally, and spiritually. Yet, through it all, she remained optimistic, determined not just to survive—but to truly thrive.

Christina came to understand that illness is not just a physical condition but often has emotional and spiritual ties. She realized that years of silencing herself to make others feel comfortable had taken a toll on her well-being. The thyroid, located in the throat—the very center of self-expression—became a symbol of her suppressed voice. She had created a space where others felt safe, but in doing so, she had neglected her own truth. Her battle with Graves' disease became a wake-up call to reclaim her voice, prioritize self-care, and nurture her emotional health.

Her journey took another profound turn when she underwent surgery to remove a large fibroid tumor that was pushing her organs out of place. This experience deepened her realization that unspoken pain and unresolved emotions could manifest physically. The tumor felt like a physical representation of the burdens she had carried for too long—years of unexpressed emotions, disappointments, and unhealed wounds.

Through it all, Christina embraced a renewed commitment to her health, recognizing that healing extends beyond medical treatment. She prioritized proper nutrition, self-care, and emotional release, understanding that true wellness is an act of love—both from God and oneself.

By sharing her journey authentically, Christina has created a space where others feel seen, heard, and understood. Her openness has resonated with many, inspiring them to listen to their bodies, honor their emotions, and walk in their truth. She is a testament to the power of faith, self-awareness, and resilience—proving that true healing is not just about overcoming illness, but about reclaiming one's wholeness.

Christina's influence extends beyond her personal story. She has taken an active role in uplifting other voices, particularly women who have faced adversity. She understands that every individual has a story worth telling and that storytelling has the power to heal, connect, and transform lives. Through her involvement with various projects and collaborations, she has worked to amplify the voices of those who have been silenced, ensuring that their stories are not only heard but valued.

Her journey has also led her to connect with like-minded individuals—women who, like her, have turned their struggles into sources of strength. She has been especially influenced by the guidance of Dr. Sue Carter-Collins, her life coach, who played a significant role in helping her heal from many traumas. Through Dr. Sue's wisdom and support, Christina gained the tools to release past wounds, embrace her true self, and step fully into her power. These connections have reinforced Christina's belief that healing and empowerment are collective efforts, and that true transformation occurs when people come together to support and uplift one another.

Despite the many challenges she has faced, Christina remains steadfast in her mission to inspire, empower, and lead with authenticity. She is not defined by her struggles but by how she has risen above them. Her journey is a powerful reminder that resilience is not about avoiding pain but about finding the strength to move through it with grace.

As she continues to share her message with the world, Christina's legacy is one of courage, faith, and unwavering determination. Her story serves as a beacon of hope, reminding others that no matter where they start, they have the power to shape their own future. She has not only embraced her worth—she has become a living testament to it, proving that when one walks in faith and purpose, they become truly unstoppable.

Her journey is far from over, and she remains dedicated to sharing her story and empowering others along the way. Those interested in learning more about her experiences can explore her memoir, *My Choice to Choose*, available on her website, **ChristinaSJohnson.com**. She also connects with her audience on Instagram **@christinjohnson** and Facebook (**Christina Johnson**), where she shares inspiration, updates, and personal insights.

For individuals passionate about interior design, Christina's firm, *Design My Investment*, specializes in bringing creative visions to life. More information about her design services can be found at **DesignMyInvestment.com**, or by following the firm on Instagram **@designmyinvestment** for the latest trends and offerings.

Additionally, those seeking unique and empowering accessories can explore Christina's line, *Jameela Jahari*, at **JameelaJahari.com**. Each piece is designed to elevate and express personal style.

Thank you for joining Christina on this journey—together, we can embrace our full potential.

JAMEELA JAHARI
BY CHRISTINA JOHNSON

DESIGN MY INVESTMENT

HOW TRICIA TRIMBLE OF SUNTEGRITY IS BREAKING NORMS IN BEAUTY

To start things off... I'm Tricia Trimble, the founder of Suntegrity. I started the brand in honor of my mother, who passed away from skin cancer. Her experience made me deeply passionate about sun protection, but I wanted to create a line of sunscreens that not only provided broad-spectrum protection, but also nourished the skin with clean, non-toxic ingredients. Suntegrity is all about merging skincare and sun care, offering mineral-based SPF products that are effective, safe, and luxurious to wear. We take a holistic approach to beauty, ensuring our formulas support skin health while being environmentally conscious.

There are so many incredible women in beauty who have paved the way for innovation and inclusivity. One that comes to mind is Tata Harper. She helped redefine luxury skincare by proving that natural, non-toxic formulations can be just as effective—if not more so—than conventional beauty products. I also admire Rose-Marie Swift, the founder of RMS Beauty, for her dedication to clean beauty long before it became mainstream. These women, among many others, have helped shift the industry towards transparency, sustainability, and high-performance natural formulations, which is something I strive for with Suntegrity as well.

At Suntegrity, we challenge the outdated idea that sunscreen is just a necessary inconvenience. Many people associate SPF with thick, greasy, or chalky formulas, and we've worked hard to create products that feel amazing on the skin while offering real skincare benefits. We're also committed to using mineral-only sunscreen filters, like non-nano zinc oxide, because we believe in providing the safest protection possible.

Another way we break norms is by focusing on education—helping people understand the long-term importance of sun protection beyond just beach days. We aim to make sunscreen a daily ritual, seamlessly integrated into skincare and beauty routines, rather than an afterthought.

I'm really proud of our two new tanning products, which use a unique natural ferment to neutralize the unpleasant scent that often comes with DHA-based self-tanners. Traditional self-tanners can have that distinctive *"fake tan"* smell due to the chemical reaction of DHA with the skin, but we wanted to create a formula that not only delivers a beautiful, natural-looking glow but also eliminates that off-putting odor.

As for what's next, we're continuing to push the boundaries of clean sun care and skin-enhancing formulations. We're always looking for innovative ways to make SPF and tanning products more enjoyable to use while staying true to our commitment to safe, effective, and skin-friendly ingredients. Expanding our lineup with multifunctional products that simplify routines without compromising on performance is a big focus for us moving forward!

I think the beauty industry is moving toward a more holistic, skin-first approach, where people prioritize products that support long-term skin health rather than just offering quick fixes. Sun protection is a huge part of that, and I expect to see even more innovation in SPF formulations that blend skincare and sun care seamlessly.

Sustainability will also continue to be a major focus—both in terms of packaging and ingredient sourcing. Consumers are becoming more conscious of their environmental impact, and brands need to respond with more eco-friendly options.

Overall, I believe the future of beauty is about transparency, efficacy, and making products that truly support people's well-being—inside and out.

CONNECT WITH TRICIA

www.suntegrityskincare.com
www.instagram.com/suntegrity

INSPIRED. EMPOWERED.
UNSTOPPABLE.

DONYALE LUNA:
THE TRAILBLAZER WHO REDEFINED BEAUTY

In an era when fashion largely overlooked Black beauty, Donyale Luna emerged as a visionary force, breaking barriers and reshaping the industry. As the first Black model to grace the cover of Vogue, Luna's influence extended far beyond the pages of magazines—she was a symbol of change, an artist in her own right, and a woman who dared to exist unapologetically in a world that was slow to embrace her brilliance.

Born Peggy Ann Freeman in 1945 in Detroit, Michigan, Luna was a dreamer from the very beginning. Her towering height, striking features, and mesmerizing presence made her unlike anyone else in her hometown. She stood out—not just because of her beauty, but because of the way she carried herself, as if she already knew she was destined for something greater.

Her rise to fame began when a photographer spotted her in Detroit. Soon after, she moved to New York, where the fashion world took notice. She changed her name to Donyale Luna, crafting an ethereal persona that blurred the lines between reality and fantasy. She wasn't just a model; she was a muse, an enigma, someone who could transform in front of the camera in a way that no one had seen before.

But America in the 1960s was not yet ready to fully embrace Luna. Though she booked work and appeared in magazines, the racial barriers in the industry were undeniable. So she did what so many trailblazers before her had done—she left. Moving to Europe, she found a world that was more willing to celebrate her uniqueness.

In 1966, Luna made history by becoming the first Black model to appear on the cover of British Vogue. It was a seismic moment, a crack in the rigid walls of an industry that had long been dominated by a singular standard of beauty. She paved the way for future icons like Naomi Campbell, Iman, and Tyra Banks. Yet, despite her success, Luna remained an outsider. She was admired but misunderstood, embraced but never fully accepted.

Her beauty was undeniable, but it was her artistry that set her apart. Luna wasn't content with just modeling—she wanted to act, to express herself, to create. She appeared in films by avant-garde directors, collaborated with artists like Salvador Dalí, and lived a life that was as unconventional as it was extraordinary. She rejected labels, refused to be confined by expectations, and lived with an almost otherworldly confidence.

But the world can be unkind to those who defy norms. Luna struggled with personal demons, and by the time she passed away in 1979 at just 33, her impact had already begun to fade from mainstream memory. The fashion industry, always moving forward, did not pause to fully recognize what she had achieved.

Today, however, her legacy is being rediscovered. In a world that now celebrates diversity in fashion, Luna's contributions are finally being acknowledged. She was ahead of her time—a pioneer who dared to redefine beauty, a woman who opened doors even as she struggled to walk through them herself. Donyale Luna was not just a model; she was a revolution.

HOW SAMANTHA GREENE IS BREAKING NORMS IN RESORTWEAR WITH TIGER AND THE MONKEY

To start things off...I am Samantha Greene, founder and designer of Tiger and the Monkey resortwear. The inspiration for the brand came to me many years ago in the North African desert when I came across three very cool nomads. That inspiration guides the style and feel of the brand until today. We thoughtfully craft pieces from both fabrics created from cutting-edge technology and those handmade by award-winning collectives to be more environmentally friendly and socially responsible. We embrace all things natural and promise to deliver premium design and quality. Our goal is to provide our customers with the sartorial means to embrace their fierce individuality in an elegant and comfortable mingling of color, print, and texture.

There are so many women, and frankly men, that inspire me in fashion. Miuccia Prada is always fashion-forward, her details and tailoring are precise and her brand really knows what it is. Ann Demeulemeester for the avant-garde and understated designs that cross lines and are feminine without being frilly. Hillary Taymour (Collina Strada) for her maximalism and the fun creative ways she turns what was previously considered to be *"junk or waste"* into works of art. Stella McCartney for challenging the fashion world to use technology to create beautiful non-animal-based products. These are just a few.

Women deserve better than the fashion they are currently being dished. Fashion and elegance can only occur if the customer is comfortable. First, that means being touched by the finest natural fabrics that breathe. For us, that is non-negotiable. It also means silhouettes that incorporate functionality and hint at your shape instead of exposing it. How about some pockets and not being squeezed like a sausage or bound around the waist? Finally, comfort is knowing what you're wearing is contributing to important progress: inflicting less damage to the environment; providing a living wage for those who have provided you with your beautiful garment, and doing your part to support and preserve ancient artisan techniques.

We've been working with one of our collectives (women-focused) recently to help introduce their textiles and craft to the US market. It takes a bit of courage to do this because it's sharing one of our Ace's, but we believe it's important to support women and their artistry and if it results in a little less attention for us, that's a price we're willing to pay. When we support one another we all succeed. As far as what's next for the brand, we are looking to expand our offerings to include shoes and jewelry, but this will take time to find the right partners/vendors who share our ethos. Patience is a virtue in this context.

I'm not someone who is very interested in trends so in terms of what is next in this space, in very simple terms, I see modern technology advancing ancient techniques. Responsible manufacturers are taking the lead on developing cutting-edge technologies to make natural fabrics less wasteful to produce and that's a win-win for everyone. In fashion, new is meeting old in exciting ways.

I hope that the trend I see towards doing less environmental damage, honoring workers, preserving the ancient handworked arts, and pushing quality above quantity continues. We should all be encouraged to recycle, upcycle, and see the beauty in what already exists. After all, fashion is cyclical and what's old always becomes new again.

CONNECT WITH SAMANTHA

www.tigerandthemonkey.com
www.instagram.com/tigerandthemonkey

The SHE RISES STUDIOS PODCAST

TUNE IN. RISE UP. THRIVE.

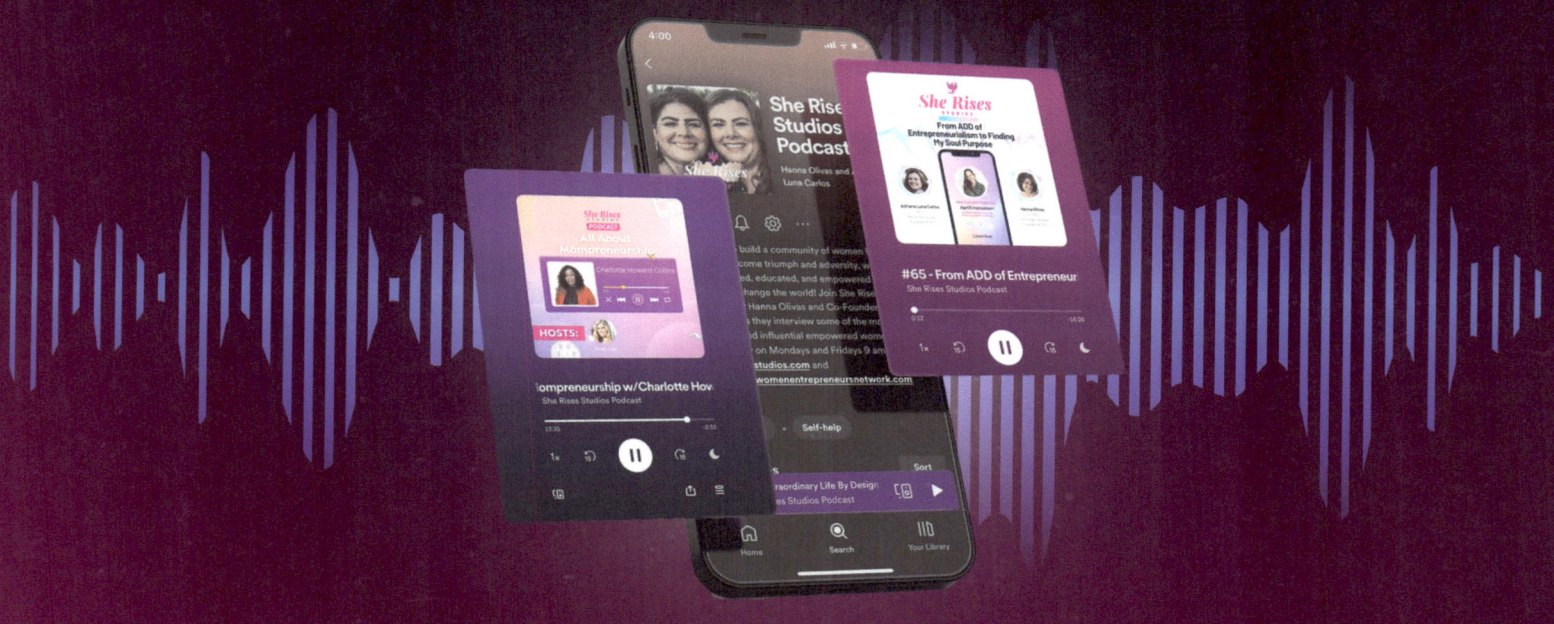

Looking for **real conversations** that inspire, empower, and ignite your potential? The **SRS Podcast** is where women like you come to **learn, grow, and rise!**

Join us for powerful **interviews with trailblazing entrepreneurs, thought leaders, and everyday women** who have turned obstacles into opportunities. Our episodes dive into:

- ➢ **Breaking through self-doubt** and stepping into confidence
- ➢ **Building a thriving business** with purpose and passion
- ➢ **Mastering work-life balance** without guilt
- ➢ **Leveling up your mindset, health, and career**
- ➢ **Finding your true purpose and living boldly**

Each episode is packed with **real stories, expert insights, and actionable strategies** to help you take your life to the next level. **This isn't just a podcast—it's your roadmap to success!**

SUBSCRIBE NOW AND START YOUR JOURNEY TO EMPOWERMENT!

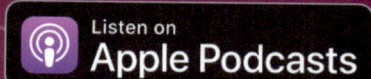

BARBARA WALTERS:
THE WOMAN WHO GAVE THE WORLD A VOICE

Barbara Walters didn't just break barriers in journalism—she shattered them. With unwavering determination and an unparalleled ability to draw out the deepest truths from the world's most powerful figures, Walters transformed the way we see television news. She wasn't just a reporter or an anchor; she was a force of nature, a trailblazer who redefined what it meant to be a woman in broadcast journalism.

Born in 1929, Walters grew up surrounded by show business. Her father, Lou Walters, was a nightclub owner and producer, giving her an early glimpse into the world of entertainment. But young Barbara was drawn not to the spotlight of the stage, but to the power of storytelling. She understood, even then, that words could change the world.

Her career began in the early 1960s at NBC's Today show, where she was initially hired as a writer and researcher. At the time, television journalism was a male-dominated field, and women were often relegated to covering topics like fashion and lifestyle. But Walters had bigger ambitions. She worked tirelessly, proving that she was not only as capable as her male colleagues but in many ways, better. By 1974, she became the first female co-host of Today, marking the beginning of her meteoric rise.

In 1976, Walters made history again when she became the first female co-anchor of a network evening news program at ABC News. Her groundbreaking $1 million contract shocked the industry, proving that women could not only hold positions of power but be compensated for them accordingly.

However, her success was met with resistance. Many of her male colleagues doubted her, dismissing her as just another *"token"* female hire. But Walters didn't just survive—she thrived.

What set Walters apart was her unparalleled interviewing style. She had a way of making people open up, of asking the questions others were too afraid to ask. From world leaders like Fidel Castro and Margaret Thatcher to pop culture icons like Michael Jackson and Oprah Winfrey, she sat across from the most influential figures of her time and made them reveal their innermost thoughts. Who could forget her tear-inducing interviews, her signature way of leaning in just enough to make even the most guarded personalities feel safe enough to be vulnerable?

In 1997, Walters co-created The View, a talk show that became a cultural phenomenon. Designed as a platform for women of different backgrounds and opinions, the show broke new ground in daytime television and continues to shape public discourse today.

Her career spanned over five decades, but Walters never lost her hunger for the story. She became synonymous with excellence, her name a gold standard in journalism. She paved the way for countless women, proving that they deserved a seat at the table—not just as reporters, but as leaders.

Barbara Walters was more than a journalist. She was a pioneer, a storyteller, and a woman who changed television forever. Her voice may be gone, but her impact will never fade.

ANNA WINTOUR:
THE VISIONARY WHO DEFINES FASHION

Few names in the fashion world command as much influence and authority as Anna Wintour. For more than three decades, she has ruled the industry with an iron will, a sharp eye, and an unparalleled ability to predict trends before they happen. As the long-time Editor-in-Chief of Vogue, Wintour has not only shaped the global fashion landscape but also transformed the way the world views fashion itself. Her signature bob, dark sunglasses, and commanding presence have made her an icon, but it is her brilliance, work ethic, and visionary leadership that have cemented her place in history.

Born in London in 1949, Anna Wintour was destined for journalism. Her father, Charles Wintour, was the editor of the Evening Standard, and from an early age, she exhibited the same determination and discipline that would later define her career. Her fascination with fashion began in her teenage years, and by the 1970s, she had worked her way into the magazine industry, holding editorial positions at Harper's Bazaar and New York Magazine. Even then, she was known for her strong opinions and an unyielding approach to excellence.

In 1988, Wintour took the helm of Vogue, a magazine that was already a powerhouse but in need of revitalization. She wasted no time in making her mark. Her very first cover—a striking image of an Israeli model wearing jeans and a high-end Christian Lacroix jacket—broke every rule. At a time when glossy, over-stylized covers were the norm, Wintour introduced an element of realness, a mix of high and low fashion that spoke to modern women. It was a bold move, but it worked. Under her leadership, Vogue became the ultimate authority in fashion, dictating what people wore, which designers thrived, and how culture and style intertwined.

Wintour's influence extends far beyond the pages of Vogue. She has championed young designers, giving them a platform that can make or break a career. Designers like Alexander McQueen, John Galliano, and Marc Jacobs have all benefited from her unwavering support. She has also played a crucial role in the evolution of The Met Gala, transforming it into the most anticipated event in the fashion world. What was once a modest fundraiser for the Metropolitan Museum of Art's Costume Institute is now an extravagant, celebrity-filled spectacle that generates millions for the museum each year.

Despite her remarkable success, Wintour has not been without controversy. Her demanding leadership style, famously depicted in The Devil Wears Prada, has led some to view her as ruthless. But those who have worked with her often describe her as a leader who simply demands the best. Her commitment to excellence has kept Vogue at the forefront of the fashion industry in an era when print media has struggled to survive. She has adapted, embraced digital platforms, and ensured that Vogue remains relevant in an ever-changing world.

Beyond fashion, Wintour is a philanthropist, supporting various causes, including AIDS research, education, and disaster relief. Her work with the CFDA/Vogue Fashion Fund has provided financial support and mentorship to emerging designers, ensuring that the industry continues to evolve.

Anna Wintour's impact is undeniable. She is more than an editor—she is a tastemaker, a power broker, and a cultural force. Her ability to balance tradition with innovation has kept her at the top for decades, and her legacy is one of influence, reinvention, and an unwavering dedication to the art of fashion.

HOW KATIE BYRNES IS REDEFINING WOMEN'S GOLF FASHION ON AND OFF THE COURSE WITH JAYEBIRD

We're proud to be expanding into more top golf shops, proving that Jayebird has a place in the best pro shops and boutiques. This June, we're launching an exciting new collection featuring innovative fabrics, classic prints, and versatile silhouettes designed to take women from the course to their everyday lives. There's so much more ahead, and we can't wait to keep pushing the boundaries of women's golf fashion.

Golf fashion is becoming more versatile, expressive, and effortless. We're seeing a shift toward bolder colors, creative layering, and sustainability-driven designs. More than anything, we hope to see greater inclusivity—where every woman feels confident and comfortable to get out and play. Golf fashion should reflect the dynamic, diverse women in the game, and Jayebird is here to lead that evolution.

To start things off...I'm the founder of Jayebird Sport, a brand I started six years ago while living in Hong Kong. Golf has been a part of my life since I was a kid, and I always dreamed of creating this brand. Jayebird is a modern golf apparel brand designed for women who want effortless style on and off the course. We blend high-performance functional golf apparel with fashion-forward designs, creating pieces that move seamlessly from the course to everyday life.

In golf, Michelle Wie West and Nelly Korda inspire me with their talent and the way they elevate the women's game. They're pushing boundaries, making golf more accessible and exciting for the next generation. In fashion, designers like Stella McCartney and Tory Burch have mastered the art of blending style with function. They prove that performance wear can be both high-fashion and practical—exactly the mindset we bring to Jayebird.

We're rethinking women's golf apparel by designing pieces that perform on the course but are stylish enough for everyday wear. Traditional golf fashion has often felt repetitive—polo after polo, skort after skort. At Jayebird, we're changing that with innovative fabrics, bold silhouettes, and luxury-inspired details. Our designs give women more versatility, so they can transition effortlessly from a round of golf to whatever comes next. It's about bringing fresh energy and individuality to the game.

CONNECT WITH KATIE

www.jayebirdgolf.com
www.instagram.com/jayebirdsport

DOROTHY DANDRIDGE: THE STAR WHO BROKE BARRIERS AND CHANGED HOLLYWOOD FOREVER

Audiences and critics alike were captivated, and the Academy took notice, nominating her for Best Actress at the 1955 Oscars. It was an unprecedented moment in Hollywood history—never before had a Black woman been recognized at this level.

Despite the nomination, the roles that followed were limited. Hollywood still struggled to see Black actresses as romantic leads, and Dandridge found herself facing the painful reality that talent alone wasn't always enough. She refused to accept roles that reinforced racial stereotypes, even though it meant fewer opportunities.

Beyond Hollywood, Dandridge's life was equally complex. She faced financial struggles, a turbulent marriage, and the challenges of raising a daughter with special needs. The racism she encountered in the industry extended beyond the screen—despite her fame, she was often denied entry to the very clubs and hotels where she performed.

By the early 1960s, her career had slowed, and her personal life was plagued with hardships. In 1965, at just 42 years old, Dandridge tragically passed away from an overdose. But while her life was cut short, her legacy endures. She proved that Black women could be more than background figures—they could be leading ladies, icons, and history-makers.

Today, Dorothy Dandridge remains a symbol of resilience, beauty, and groundbreaking achievement. She walked so others—like Halle Berry, Viola Davis, and Lupita Nyong'o—could run. Hollywood still has progress to make, but thanks to women like Dorothy, the doors are forever open.

Dorothy Dandridge was more than just a beautiful face or a captivating voice—she was a pioneer, a woman who refused to be confined by the racial limitations of her time. As the first Black woman to be nominated for an Academy Award for Best Actress, she shattered Hollywood's glass ceiling and paved the way for future generations of Black performers. But her journey was not an easy one. It was filled with triumphs, heartbreak, and an unwavering determination to be seen, not just as a Black actress, but as a leading lady in her own right.

Born in 1922 in Cleveland, Ohio, Dandridge's early years were shaped by both talent and adversity. Her mother, Ruby Dandridge, was an actress, and from a young age, Dorothy and her sister Vivian were pushed toward the stage. Performing as *"The Wonder Children,"* the girls toured the country, showcasing their singing and dancing skills. While these experiences honed Dorothy's performance abilities, they also exposed her to the harsh realities of racism in America.

As she grew older, Dorothy and Vivian formed the Dandridge Sisters, a jazz trio that performed at prestigious venues like the Cotton Club in Harlem. But Dorothy's ambition extended beyond the stage—she wanted to be a movie star. She longed for roles that reflected her talent and complexity, rather than the stereotypical maid or servant characters typically offered to Black actors in the 1930s and 1940s.

Her breakthrough came in 1954 with Carmen Jones, a film adaptation of the opera Carmen, where she played the fiery and seductive lead. Her performance was mesmerizing—equal parts strength and vulnerability, sensuality and sorrow.

www.sherisesstudios.com

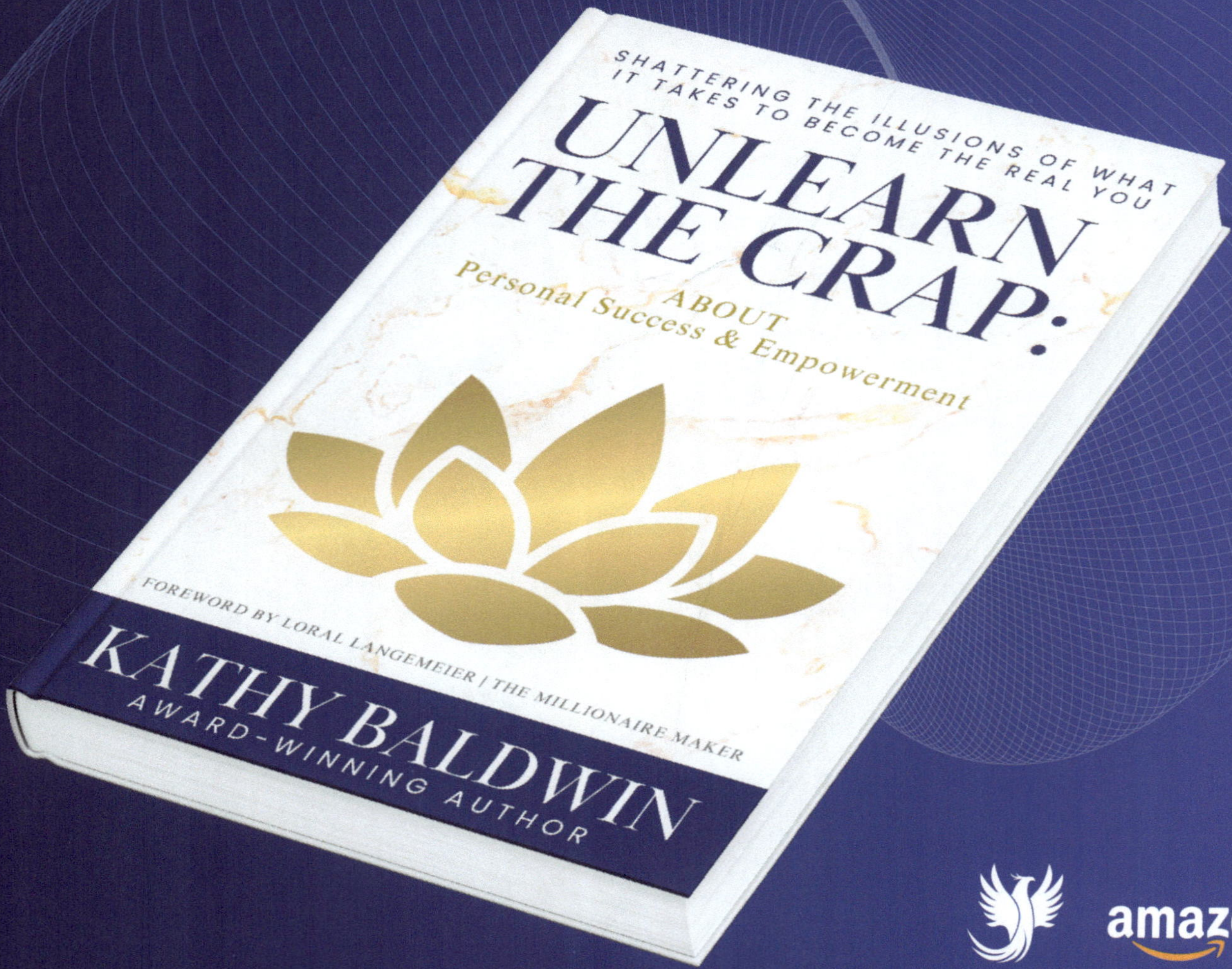

SHE RISES
S T U D I O S

*U*NLEASH YOUR STORY
BECOME A PUBLISHED AUTHOR!

Have you ever dreamed of sharing your wisdom, experience, or passion with the world? **Now is your time!**

Publishing a book isn't just about writing—it's about **establishing your authority, inspiring others, and creating a lasting legac**y. Plus, with the **$138.5 billion book industry** booming, there's never been a better moment to step into the spotlight.

At **SRS Publishing**, we don't just publish books—we **elevate voices, empower authors, and create change-makers**. Our mission is to help women break barriers, amplify their stories, and thrive in the publishing world. Whether you're an entrepreneur, thought leader, or storyteller at heart, **we're here to guide you every step of the way.**

JOIN THE FASTEST-GROWING PUBLISHING HOUSE FOR WOMEN IN THE USA.

READY TO TURN YOUR DREAM INTO REALITY?

 www.SheRisesStudios.com | contact@sherisesstudios.com